THE STRANGE YEARS OF MY LIFE

COMPARATIVE VIEW
OF THE HEIGHTS OF THE
PRINCIPAL MOUNTAINS &c.
IN THE
WORLD.

THE STRANGE YEARS OF MY LIFE

NICHOLAS LAUGHLIN

PEEPAL TREE

First published in Great Britain in 2015
Peepal Tree Press Ltd
17 King's Avenue
Leeds LS6 1QS
UK

ISBN 13: 978184522924

Supported using public funding by
ARTS COUNCIL
ENGLAND

For my parents, who have almost always said yes

CONTENTS

When did we ever write so much
as since the beginning of our Civil Wars?

— *Montaigne*

1   *Species the maps don't know*

EVERYTHING WENT WRONG

Don't mention my name in your letters.
Don't write down my address.
In fact, better not write letters at all.
Better no one knows that you can write.

You'll know not to drink the water.
You'll know not to travel by night.
Don't carry foreign banknotes.
Never give your name when you pay the bill.

You will need a shot at the border.
The needles are perfectly safe.
Yellow fever can't be allowed to pass.
I knew a man who died in just three days.

The weather turned truly nasty.
It flooded ten miles around.
A boat capsized. A box was swept away.
I couldn't afford to bribe the customs guard.

Don't trust the maps: they are fictions.
Don't trust the guides: they drink.
In this country there's no such thing as "true north."
Don't trust natives. Don't trust fellow travellers.

Better no one knows you sleep alone.
Already no one remembers you at home.

LES RENDEZVOUS

Inspector Slimane brings the newspapers himself.
We all know there is a spy in every café,
and an almost-safe house in the Rue de l'Hôtel du Miel.

You don't like to boast. Thirty-three daylight robberies,
six blackmailings, one white glove of diamonds,
machine guns, a car chase, and two million gone.

Roubles, you mean. You change them with the *tailleur*
in the Rue de l'Impuissance.
You take your time.

Mirrors break. Guns go off by themselves.
Doors open and close, no one knows why,
or how the strychnine got in the Spaniard's coffee.

You bring the newspapers yourself, Pierrot.
You wait in the third café on the Rue de l'Homme à la Perle,
your back to the door.

You feel quite at home. No one admits he knows your name.
The waiters are your friends, the police are your friends,
your enemies are your friends.

Even your friends are your friends
at the Café des Rendezvous.

VILLA-LOBOS AMONG THE CANNIBALS

There are good Germans and bad Germans.
He could have been one of us.

EL SUR

The four cardinal points are left and right.
My shoulder has freckled overnight:
bears and dogs and ploughs.
The French discover Australia.
Letters from the New World.
Hydrogen rhymes with gold.
A name for this new science.
Good weather for armies to drown.
The four cardinal points are close and wrong.

LAMPS, CLOCKS, MIRRORS, MAPS

Lamps, clocks, mirrors, maps,
etc., props all drowsy with dusk.
The windows roped open, the breeze outside
launching brief arias of leaves and plastic bags.

I found your list snug in an unread book
(no one reads poems, no book could be safer),
the names crossed out.

         So many maps –
islands, boroughs, bridges, trees,
towers, colours, thumbprints, hills,
rings of stones and single stones,
and the paths of particular citizens:
the certain, the gentle, the wary young,
men with ladders, women with ropes –
creased, pinpricked, stained.

With every unfolding the patient city outside
rewords itself: a street revealed,
a park unleashed, a fountain wheels.
You are still making your way back home,
errands remembered, and look how it hasn't rained.
Near the river: birds,
a species the maps don't know.

THE GAMBLER'S SONG

Letters get lost in the Century Hotel,
where some rooms share numbers,
some rooms share doors,
some rooms have neither.

READING HISTORY

The time was a page on which too much had been written,
in the racing hands of too many months and years.
Names of correspondents, station names,
dates of conversations, book reviews,
fragments of memoirs, directions to new hotels.
Mais que suis-je venu faire sur cette Terre?
And lives of pianists and architects and saints.
And the page was creased with too many hurried unfoldings.

And the houses grumbled with the weight of lists and pages.
The scent of lilies, the drawl of lazy études.
It took longer to read about those months than to live them.
"It astonished me that my friends could be so forgiving."
"I was certain those meetings in April could never be repeated;
November proved me wrong." "I was surely lucky,
for S———— had told no one else about my discovery."
"I was right." "It was there." "It had gone." "I was barely mistaken."

"We never read so much as we did on that visit.
We can have done nothing but read the entire week.
We walked in the afternoons, but even then
all we talked about was what we were reading."
A generation decided together in silence
to have done with fiction and to renounce the stage.
Nothing seemed lost. Everyone kept a diary.
Every remark or detail was preserved in their letters.

Three piano notes came drifting through the house
like yellow leaves, then the curtain swept them away.
No, they came like footsteps that hesitate,
or three pages that slowly turn in the evening draught.
He watched the pages turn and history begin.
Already many hands were crossing and tracing
in the steelpoint light of many jars of ink.
Three leaves fell, and already too much had been written.

2   *Because I have a hard time sitting still*

MY TRAITORS

My traitors were my lovers.
I was the Aztec Kid.
I was the night captain on the S.S. *Escape*,
here today, French tomorrow.

My dangers were my friends.
Easy come, easy bruise,
old odds, new tricks.
That was then,

nightfaster.
Now I sweat cold gin.
I call for more ice.
I cover the mirror before I sleep.

ALL THIS WAY

Those quarter-hearted months learning Chinese.
Trading last year's currencies.
Drinking evidence dissolved in coffee.

Those months of wrong days.
Those months not far enough away.
Those months of my own name.

Self-portrait not knowing what comes next.
Self-portrait forgetting my lines.
Self-portrait with no excuse.

I never thought I'd make it to the border.
I never thought I'd hold my breath so long.
I never thought I would come all this way
to come all this way.

GRINGO TOUJOURS

Because I have a hard time sitting still.
Rumours about my behaviour.
The malice of my friends.
Because this kind of weather does not end.

Days long as mistakes,
weeks boring as rain,
the acres of my bed,
sheets that itch like paper,

electric fish, lantern boats,
tepid decaf river.
I wrap my fever in paper,
I sweat like milk and glass and red cayenne.

Tattoo, sunburn, vaccination scar,
sweat and freckle in my sleep.
Because I have been wanted and disowned.
Everything is easier far from home.

SELF-PORTRAIT IN THE NEOTROPICS

Eleven of the strange years of my life.
Months on end I lived on tapioca,
I lived on mud and permanganate broth,
and river water red as rum,
bivouacked with rainflies
and fire ants and sundry native guides.
The parrots already knew some French.
Nous sommes les seuls français ici.
Call it sunstroke, *le coup de bambou.*
I came all this way with half a plan,
an extra handkerchief, and Humboldt (abridged).
Here I lack only the things I do not have.

Eleven years of untimely weather,
earthquakes and fireflies and mud.
The colonel writes his complaints to the general.
The general writes his complaints to the emperor.
The emperor writes to Jesus Christ,
who damns us all.
Nous sommes les seuls français left in the world.
I came all this bloody way
to sit in a cheap café with bandaged hands.
I translate detective novels, Dr. Janvier.
It keeps me in *dinero*, out of trouble.
I miss only the friends I do not have.

CHINESE WHISPERS

Amours de voyage, Chinese whispers,
noms de plume on *le téléphone arabe,*
shredded poems, intercepted codes,
crossword limericks, sonnet cryptograms.

Stop. You have made a blunder.
Stop. I act on the best advice.
Stop. Decide at once.

I speak six human languages,
I know my way around the souk.
But I am no anthropologist.

Yours was the purer French.
Mine was the ruse.

I am your double agent.
I am my own false hope.
Stop. I am held against my will.

I know my way around.
Beware the Trojans, *stop,*
bribe the Greeks.

MY BEAUTIFUL FRIENDS

My dears, honest people, customs guards,
lawyers, joiners, engineers,
bakers, cub reporters, aunts and thieves,
senators, our hero, artists, quacks,
shysters, muggers, doctors, Portuguese.

My beautiful famous friends.

In those days all the spies were trained as poets.
I mean the other way around.
We were all trained in stagecraft and explosives,
metrics, marksmanship, cryptics, and poisons.
Aliases. Astronomy. Crown of thorns.

What use these grammars now?
In this wrong country,
in these wrong days.

The title of my memoir is *Spilt Milk*.

My beautiful harmless friends,
do not feel comforted,
do not feel saved.

Still, still, the same, the same.

JE VOUS ÉCRIS DU BOUT DU MONDE

Damn these fevers. Damn these speechless days.
Damn my old friends.

Damn my gambled treasures.
My frogsuit of jade.
My eighteen leopards.
My pretty crown of thorns.

There are only twenty-nine hours in every day,
only sixteen months in a year,
I only have twelve lives.

Damn this country, pretty on the map,
frontiers of crinkled scarlet.

There are too many wrong countries in the world.

I did not invent the magic lantern.
I did not invent the hot-air balloon.

There is only one day in every day.

ENOUGH IS ENOUGH

I am waiting on your letter.
When it comes I will read it like it is written on your skin,
like it is written on a crust of bread.

If you saw me now you would not know me,
my face stained brown, my hands scored with scars,
my back tattooed with intimate anagrams.

The name of this place tastes like a bit lip.
My ninety-seven words of French are no good to me now,
my tongue tied up in the local accent.

I still have good intentions,
second-best of hopes,
three quarters of a heart.

Dear John, enough is enough.
Please come home.
Nothing is forgiven.

3   *Your accent is wrong*

BON COURAGE

Aha: so I suspected.
The maps are blank.
Ants have been at work.
Librarians have sat up through the night,
erasing.

And this is not a diary, acrobat.
Stop looking for my name.

A PLACE TO START

Imaginary spiders drinking real tea.
Imaginary parrots drinking real milk.

SELF-PORTRAIT AS LAST CITIZEN OF THE ISLAND

Exiled by a congress of tides,
the trucial powers of salt,
the perfect seal of the sea.
This would be April if months still had names.

The island is a red egg in the sea.
Red flags in the almond trees.
Red brigade of hermit crabs,
and the red squadrons of salt-scavenging bees.
And my red salty eyes.

Citizen, brother, traitor:
raw as bait.
The Trades' reprieve:
too late.

L'heure midi plus sonore qu'un moustique.
A census of the sands.
A tongue too salt to speak.
Ransom of brine.

Citizen, ambassador,
at last I know nothing
under this salt-white sky.
At last the sea is only the sea.

Still,
boy, your accent is wrong.

SUB ROSA

What starts in the tepidarium
will end in my memoirs.
As many regrets as friends.
As many friends as second thoughts
as bad mistakes.
I was born too young. I came the wrongside way.

I have had many third thoughts, fourth guesses,
five parts gin.
My gasoline days.
— I hate to make a mess
but I do what I have to do.

I was there when they raised the flag.
My name was on the list, Pierrot. I never took the oath.
I did my time.
I did your time.
I wear the same tattoo.

— But who do I fool.
The accent gives me away.
Hence the funny walk, hence the wince.

FURTHER MISTAKES

Party trick with tuning fork,
finger, and rubber band.

Self-portrait with bloody lip
and bandaged hand.

Plans nobody makes,
weather that only smells like rain,
the spare clock that needn't be wound.

Lost key to a room where nobody sleeps.
Mirror with black spots.
A single empty cup.

No, it is full of lukewarm tea.
No, it is cracked and home to a spider
praying to its own saint.

I pray to my own saint.

Still life with porcelain
and ransom note and sand.

MR. KEATS HAS LEFT HAMPSTEAD

He scribbled notes to the bees,
he dropped little flags of paper about the lawn,
and the bookcase was crammed with leaves,

tiny stars exploded in his lungs,
Rigel and Betelgeuse,
tiny roses eating up his veins,

like any orphaned bird, he chose
a suit of nails,

and he wrote his name over and over and over,
so I write his name over and over and over.

NEWS FROM ROME

The rumour that you are dead.
Limbs stitched into your bed.
The furniture chopped and burned.

Severn destroys the umpteenth draft of his letter.

A letter to London takes one month.
A letter to me takes 194 years.

LONGTEMPS

Hemlock and sinew and screw.
Lung and tongue and bruise.
Baritone in furs.

My handwork and my heartwork
and my keatswork. Lost shirt,
fresh moustache.

Dear enemy, dear heart,
dear throat, dear ark.
Baritone wants his bowl of milk.

Dear August, lost pearls,
silk and sweat and fur.
Baritone walking in his sleep.

ARS POETICA

There are guns to clean,
there is fish to wrap.

4   *The answer is strange*

BOTANY

Plant these seeds so you can tend a forest
so you can long for a stranger to feed the wild birds.

RAIN

Rain, so I dream of rain,
like a new history for a conquered kingdom.
Perhaps we'll learn to live in cathedrals of rain,
running gently as though we are running on glass.
Washed in lovely acids, we turn silver and rose,
and the rain makes stains like the wrong chemical on film.

Rain like waiting, prayer-beads of patience
strung from the sky. Before we speak we need quiet.

Rain and the phones go dead.
Rain and a mouth is drinking, so it cannot speak.
Rain and children run the other way
(gently, as if on glass),
forgetting the message you bribed them to deliver.

Rain and accents sound strange
and a stranger leans in slightly too close to listen
and mishears a story about a fictional journey
and buys maps and sells his house and changes his life, but blame the rain.

Rain and a distant traveller has missed his plane,
his plane goes round and round and round and round in the rain.

I DISCOVER I AM RUSSIAN

I discover I have a Russian heart.
I discover I am a small boy with a heart full of stones,
a bag of stones.
They click like the heartbeat of a clock.
In Russia this is how we sleep,
the small weights of our hearts shifting from left to right,
sliding and clicking as we tumble through the night.

In Russia our livers are carved of petrified wood
and our lungs are stuffed with black moss.
Iciest water climbs and falls in our veins,
salt meeting cold with small electric shivers,
tinkling the wet stones of our hearts.

In Russia when I am in love
my heart crashes terribly against my ribs,
wonderful they do not crack.
In Russia when I am in love
one by one I press the stones of my heart
into a birch-twig sling, but they don't fly far.

In Russia I walk for ten miles every day
when the sun rises at midnight
over a minor planet of salt.
When the sun rises at noon,
I walk only as far as I can sling a stone.

CLUES

A flower named for a bird.
A bird swooping like rain.
Rain the size of an island.
An island creased like my hand.
My hand hot as my tongue.
My tongue new as a flower.

A leaf clean as a feather.
A feather drenched like string.
String to tie up a map.
A map smudged by my fingers.
My fingers in my teeth.
My teeth tearing a leaf.

Your skin furred like a flower.
Your neck aloof as a bird's.
Your eyes like spirals of rain.
Your body unknown as an island.
A blush as hot as your hands.
A secret like your tongue.

AFTER EIGHT DAYS

After eight days
and eight different kinds of weather,
the usual bouts of hunger and thirst and patience and sleeping,
four little pills have undone me
(call them here and this and now and now)

and my heart is a falling bird
tumbling in air,
and my lungs like two stones
have sunk to the tide,
and like a leaf dropped eight days dry
I rust, I fold.

Here is a photograph of you:
after eight days your face should not be strange.
Here is what your arms felt like last time:
my body should not be so strange.

A hand is a trap made of little bones.
A ring is a story half-told.
A shirt is a riddle about your heft, your smell.
Eight days is a riddle about the world.
The answer is strange.

I THINK I AM BECOMING MYSELF

My clock like a heart –
I mean my heart like a clock.
Is counting the minutes like second thoughts.
Hours are sore like a cramp.
Days are quick like a twitch in the ribs.
So a body takes its time.

I am becoming thirty-two years old.
Nice to, at last, be strange.

I mean my heart like a heart, stubborn and strange,
asking no questions, doing its job,
counting its seconds in electric gulps.

To please my hardworking heart
I gulp water, coffee, wine:
chemistry. Alchemy. Electrophoresis.
My blood runs to gold and back.
My blood runs to milk and back.

Like a twitch in my bones, my marrow discovers true north.
Like a hum in my heart, electromagnetic thirst.
My compass like a heart –
I mean my heart.

I am thirty-two years old all over the world.

WHEN I SAID "MY HEART"

I meant *my heart*,
blind as all meat,
caught in a hug,
shoving away,
going nowhere.

RIDDLE

Here is a small painting about the world.
Here is a black mirror to be heard.

This house is unfinished business for you.
Here is a fourth chance to dream of this room,

a fifth chance. This may last for years,
or maybe just while sleep is so near.

Here are the vowels fresh as I said,
ripe with hardly a purple scent,

and here is a whole book to help you say.
Here is one more chance just in case.

IF YOU CAME HERE LOOKING FOR THE NEWS

What I would tell you is what I would tell myself
if I wasn't there.

It was five directions at a time
and only one magnet.

THE WAKER'S SONG

In my January bed
I knit like a bone
until I am a creature twice my size.

5   *Birds do not yet have names*

BODIES OF THE SAINTS

Flowers: so their lips, their nacred
auricles, their burning finger-
tips: they show us first how flesh
is holy incandescence, our flesh
too (foreheads pressed to hips,
to thighs, to knees), the smudge of blue
and scent of roses, turpentine,
we carry after in our skin
(and other relics smuggled in:
their torn shirts, kerchiefs soiled),
each scrap of paper (clean as flesh)
illumined by their silence, how
they make of breathing wanting, make
of wanting grace: so we are martyrs
now to craving, we ignite
and all complacence burns away
till pure and blossoming we stay,
insatiable we moan and hymn
and pray: at last, sublime, we take
unsolace of their silvered limbs:
at their altars, naked, stand:
they are burning in our hands.

I am sometimes a cloud waiting behind your eyes,
I am made of small ants of remembered light,
perhaps you see me when you are falling asleep,
sailing like a holiday constellation,
Antares and Betelgeuse and Mars.
I am sometimes a bruise on your knee or shin,
a smear of new mud or roucou pulp,
scent of cinnamon, rooibos, paprika,
I am made of powdered rust and a little sweat,
maybe I am magnetic, or hum in the dark,
or shimmer like smoke from a kermes pyre.
Maybe I am sea-water opaque with salt,
Sargasso tea. Maybe the taste of me stings,
maybe I am sweet as a ferrous broth.
Maybe I am a ruse of retiring day,
a blush of farewell madder, something half-glimpsed
before the light moves on. A strobe-lit finger,
wet. A rumpled scarf. A glistening lip.
A spattered kerchief that will not wash out,
a pattern like a pause of little ants,
scent of mace. I am sometimes a newborn nerve,
a tiny coil of glass and neon and heat,
an evening thunderstorm inside a vein,
a tiny nova when you are falling asleep.

DEUX LAPINS

The rabbit of the Andes and the rabbit of Sar-e-Sang,
eager to see the world, these little lords,
touring the volcanoes, insist a daily swim
to the true marine, these icy little twins,
and their eyes are glass of gold, fire-blue,
veins of angels, the virgin's shawls and cloths,
her counting-beads, O Wilton, O Tibet,
O copper, jade, enamel, little saints,
roses for the rabbits of the mountains, purses of blood,
spendthrift travellers, Berbice indigo,
Lincoln woad, a parcel of hot pebbles,
a gem for each ear, each violet-embroidered glove,
O vanitas, a mirror cut from blue stone
staring into its own pure veins alone.

Never call it magic.
                    From a hat,
a wren, another wren.
(Scarves. Eggs. Balls of glass.)
This is my perfect trick.

A bird in the hand is a scar in the hand.

A hare is another trick, a worry that runs.
This makes sense but for the German tongue.

                              *

A fur purse for blood, a trick spun out of nerves.
A creature of steel and insomnia, little coils,
hot, hot little eyes.

A hare has won the race to martyrdom.

My wrenship, my badge, my spurs,
my ambush and wake.

Birds do not yet have names.

LES ARGOTIERS

Acrobat's false beard.
Baritone's false hat.
Dr. Janvier is my "real name."

Serious business.
Vaccination scar.
Fellow craft.

Continentals. Federales.
Agents of the crown.
Cyanide thieves.

Out here in the colonies
we're all just cousins.

Acrobat says: we are cleared for flight.

My suitor expected
a torso inside a whale.
Drained his tub
yelling and dried his hands.

STRANGE CURRENCIES

River traffic, sea traffic,
heart traffic, lung traffic,

head trade, heart trade,
hand trade, gun trade,

heart wars, night wars,
river wars, rum wars,

night saints, blood saints,
gun saints,

knife lessons, knife tricks,
night tricks,

night sleep, milk sleep,
river sleep.

I saw it myself, the sun that dropped
in a lake of blue milk.
A blue god, bird-mantled,
sweating honey.
Golden captain, Christmas astronaut,
dropping like a pearl,
and the highest air, hot glass,
sticky horizon. I saw it myself,
I have blue milk on my hands,
doubting Matthew, doubting Jude.

A LEGEND

In the cup of milk that spills at the wrong man's feet,
I am in those minerals, those sugar chalks,
those blind potassiums. I am those balms
that spill for the wrong man. I am that honey
buried in the ground and baked in rock,
and permanent. If you believe
in the geological patience of bees,
how long it takes to build a planet,
how long it takes to put away the hydrogen
to build a sun. If you believe
the job of bees is not to bury honey.
The job of a sun is not to make light
but to burn itself out.
The job of milk is to swallow sugar,
and spill itself at some man's feet,
extravagant. If you believe
it is always the wrong man.
But I am those balms.

THE DREAMERS

I sleep like a swimmer
who has not yet learned to swim.

*

I sleep like a drowned man
who has not yet drowned.

ACCIDENT OF BIRDS

As if a riddle for the saints,
careless in your net of wings,
accident of birds.
I hitch my shirt of scars and fur.
Your feathers bit in gravity's
machine, the toothed wheels of the world.

One cog cries, another holds
its breath, the chain of tides cracks free,
the Andes jostle China, Indus
stalls, Euphrates spins confused.

Hushed by the shadows of many birds,
the height where all stars intersect,
our knees set, our tongues out,
gaping, ready to fall, to fall.

6   *Small Husband*

SELF-PORTRAIT AT THE START OF THE RAINY SEASON

Suddenly my hair grows like a weed,
squirming, so I cannot sleep at night,
all this swimming makes my eyes turn green,

until morning, trembling through the house,
swallowing a thirst I cannot fill,
through the rooms the mirrors pale and cloud,

in my cave of glass I boil, I rage,
weather pounds against the leaking windows,
this is my tide of thriving, week of grace,

cling the heart of this round bell of bone,
hum each echo in the sodden air,
gulping at the world, its drowning bowl.

Drenched, the wren, a twist of fur and twigs,
furious in the cold teeth of the rain,
a gasp and two hot eyes that blink and blink.

MY PREY, MY TWIN

Little king, my prey, my twin,
trail of pearls in the grass.

Glass bones in my wrist.
Pulse in a maze of glass.

All throat and eye
and wrist and spy,
electric ribs.
Trick as a trap.

My nettle tongue prickled with a pledge.
The crook of my arm pricked with the pulse of a bird.

SMALL HUSBAND

Mercy on My Small Husband

Mercy on my small husband.
When he sleeps bare five hours a night
wrapped in paper like an accident,
like an insect itching serifs inside an envelope.
He sleeps knowing I am nowhere near.
He sleeps near I know not where.
My small husband is an impossible sleeper.

Sleep is not impossible.
I cough and scrabble my blanket of fur,
my bed of cold white zinc.
And above me is all the clean glass air, safe from echoes.
Unmercied, I am bound in my own veins.
I keep my watch like a leftover promise,
staring at Orion's crotch,
at the stumbling of the blind bull.
No one will surprise my small husband,
not me.

My little king,
and all his armies when they rose,
the thousand eyes, the thousand wings,
one heart too great for me.
Night's armada hunts to west,
animals and ships, ten thousand lights,
reel to his cry, parade to his permanent eye.

Burn as I do, I cannot watch forever,
small husband, flesh as mine is not sublime
or permanent, ransom to your height,
temper to the furnace of your too-endless night,
tempted and sold and too slowly cold.
Rust and a hand'swidth of earth.
Small husband, I am eager to be patient.
Can there be enough of me to wait.
Now I am the impossible waker.

My Head Was Too Big

My head was too big.
Then I had not learned to swim.
(Now I swim as a stone.)
One, two, three, four, wait, six, seven, eight,
my veins for a moment turned to glass,
scarlet craquelure.

The ambush of my small husband.
My lord said: Do not wait. Do not measure.
Champion and tryst.

A crown for my small husband.
His duchy needing a name.
The new interregnum of lust.
Constellations come to truce.
Small husband, I can be hungrier than this.

Hardly bargained,
              small husband,
it seems I am marked as yours.
Your name frecked on my shoulder,
hieroglyph of melanin and bruise.
I sweat, small husband, like your gold.

My small husband's corkscrew is my spine.
Small husband, you have tricked me like a bee.
My romans and my germans
and my birdgroom for a spy,
electric ribs,
pearly and clean.
You are not mine.

Wordless as a Surgeon

Wordless as a surgeon, small husband,
you are too hard on me.
I mean you are not hard enough.

Small husband, I am too intact,
every bone too neatly sewn
to every bone.
I have not known your flinch.

These pebbles I swallow are too small,
my lusts are too small,
my lungs are too pretty, purple and rose,
small husband, come with angry teeth,
I am nothing that cannot (or if I cannot) be torn.

Small husband, I will be yeast and seed
if you will be strange in your appetite.

Small as I am of living, of longing,
small as I am of what I ask, paper flowers & delicate paper fronds,
my prayers too small, my pride too small,
the hairspring of my wrist & my paper heart too small,
small husband, will you ask too much of me,
come like too much asked.

Lord, if nothing else do not explain.
Lord, I will ask for nothing else.
Someday I may be famous for my hunger.

Something on the Governor's Head

Something on the governor's head.
My small husband perched like a smart of salt,
like a gasp, but not for my lungs.
My small husband coughs and it is honey.
When will I be the lemon of your tongue, little king.
Blushes and knots and sweats,
a lingering taste of rust,
embroidery of thirst,
my throat stitched tight.

My good shoulder frecked with scars,
my good mouthful of stones,
my good swim *dans tout ce lait d'eau vive,*
my good end.
Not, small husband, yet,
not yet.
My small husband breaks my vow of silence.

Your alias, small husband,
the password of your name,
key to the melting of lakes, the opening of gates,
your name like the crack of metal, St. Somewhere's fire,
St. Someone's dance, a shiver quicker than silver,
my quicks and my quirks and my nerves hotter than silver.

Your electric names.
Astronomies and theorems and slangs.
Graces and mercies.
Arums and Bethlehem-stars.
Volcanoes and lightning.
The invention of glass.
Your name like glass in my mouth, little king,
silver and glass.
Your name like the whole world inside my mouth.
I never speak. I never ask.

ROITELET

Small husband, I have been longing for you,
parched and hugging my tinder heart.
This afternoon too tranced and hot,
dusk too cautious and hot and silent,
night reluctant, each hot hour
holding its breath, what is it waiting to hear?

Small husband, you hide among the ants,
you wait among the thorns, your eyes green as the setting sun,
a heartbeat hunting a red stone under the leaves,
electroplectic fidget.
Small husband, is this where you will drink?

Small husband, I too sleep alone,
tied to myself, limb to limb to limb,
a hitch of grass and hair and string,
weighed in the earth of my bed, cold and red.

Small husband, I too never sleep
in the loud night, the night like a bed of stone,
each star like a pebble flung to glass.

Small husband, you watch at dawn,
you call like a necklace of cold water in the rocks,
raincloud in your throat, a song like drowning,
breath battling the dark drag of desire,
a song of names that cannot be pronounced or repeated.

Small husband, I want to follow you
up the scarlet ladder of your throat,
the thread you snag from leaf to leaf
with knots to show I cannot follow on,
a shivering string that snags too in my wrist.

My little king,
I dream you crouch in my thighs and watch through my eyes
the failed flight of my hands,
you creep in my shirt and your claws clutch tight in my lungs
so I breathe in winces, like a bird.

Small as you are,
small husband,
is there room in your breast for me,
a sprout of green,
for a long mystery, a great fire,
an arrow, an echo,
a story,
a solstice,
tomorrow.

HIS MAGNITUDES

My small husband in his magnitudes,
his high equator and his noose of pearls
– alpha, beta, gamma –
anagram or map or torrid zone.
For me there is no rescue in the stars.
Only I am sunburnt of his brag,
pricked with ginger.

Plaything, empearled,
my small husband's whim
down my bloodstream in electric gold,
ransom for his stars and in my veins.
Caution, pericardium,
femur, watch for danger,
my small husband's siege will not be long.

ACKNOWLEDGEMENTS

I'm not a slow writer, but I'm a sometimish one. The poems assembled here were written over nearly a decade and a half, in erratic starts and (mostly) stops. During this time, a surprising number of friends and colleagues read various batches of these poems and offered encouragement, always gratefully received, and advice, not always heeded. For their attention, insight and kindness, I wish to thank, in something like chronological order: Anu Lakhan; Mary Adam; Jeremy Taylor; Vahni Capildeo; Brendan de Caires; Ian McDonald; Anne Walmsley; Edward Baugh; Mervyn Morris; Kei Miller; Vivek Narayanan; and Andre Bagoo.

In 2007 I received the Rex Nettleford Fellowship in Cultural Studies from the Rhodes Trust, for a literary research project that I still consider a work in progress. I hope it's some small consolation to the selection committee to know that the reading, travelling, and musing I did with the support of the fellowship contributed to a number of the poems in this book – though probably in no way they would have anticipated.

Many of these poems, or versions of them, were previously published in print or online journals. My thanks to the editors of the following publications: Robert Minhinnick, *Poetry Wales*; Nicolette Bethel, *tongues of the ocean*; Michael Hulse, *The Warwick Review*; Ralph Wessman, *Famous Reporter*; Alex Houen, *Blackbox Manifold*; Vivek Narayanan, *Almost Island*; Roberta James, *Magma*; Libby Hodges and Abby Sugar, *St. Petersburg Review*; Bernardine Evaristo, *Poetry Review*; also Ian Dieffenthaller and Anson Gonzalez, editors of the anthology *100 Poems from Trinidad and Tobago*.

And particular thanks to Jeremy Poynting and Hannah Bannister of Peepal Tree Press – longtime colleagues – for their patience and practical generosity. A poet's most tangibly significant support comes from the brave publisher who commits time, thought, and money to make possible a book. I am grateful for theirs.

ABOUT THE AUTHOR

Nicholas Laughlin is a writer and editor. He was born in Trinidad and has always lived there.

He is the editor of *The Caribbean Review of Books* and the arts and travel magazine *Caribbean Beat*; programme director of the Bocas Lit Fest, Trinidad and Tobago's annual literary festival; and co-director of the contemporary art space and network Alice Yard.

He has edited a volume of early essays by C.L.R. James, *Letters from London* (2003), and a revised, expanded edition of V.S. Naipaul's early family correspondence, *Letters Between a Father and Son* (2009).

MORE RECENT POETRY FROM TRINIDAD

Vahni Capildeo
Utter
ISBN: 9781845232139; pp. 78; pub. 2013; price: £8.99

In *Utter* the reader is transported by image and sound into a universe where there appear to be no limits to what the imagination is capable, and Vahni Capildeo relishes the freedoms inherent in such a world. Old boundaries come down: between the past and present, between human and animal, animate and inanimate, between the Caribbean and the global elsewhere, between the experienced world and the world of books. Rooted in an energetic sense of history, her vision remains scrupulously contemporary, wholly engaged in our present moment with poems triggered by the earthquake in Haiti, the politics of the globalized Antilles, and the islands' industrial and agricultural contradictions. And even when the past is evoked, it remains wonderfully modern: dead soldiers welcoming a modern English apartment-dweller; Beowulf-era abandoned women pinned and pining on islands or beneath trees and recent migrants travelling their transatlantic journeys. And for all this, there live moments of community and tenderness, beauty and humour, all borne by her witty, prodigious intelligence. This is a book that rewards multiple readings, for at each reading some new untold treasure is sure to be discovered and rediscovered, making it a book as unexpected and as compendious as life.

Find this and well over a hundred collections of Caribbean poetry for secure ordering on www.peepaltreepress.com
Email orders@peepaltreepress.com,
or phone us on +44 (0)113 245 1703